STONES

Rescued From Shame

SAYO AKINTOLA

COVENANT PUBLISHING

Stones: Rescued From Shame
Sayo Akintola

Unless otherwise stated, all scripture quotations are taken from the Holy Bible, King James Version (KJV). Other versions cited are NIV, NKJV, NASB, TS98, TJB and WEB.

ISBN 978-1-907734-16-8

First Edition, First Printing October 2016

Covenant Publishing
samadewunmi@btinternet.com

Covenant Publishing is part of New Covenant Church
Charity Registered in England & Wales number 1004343
Registered Address: 506-510 Old Kent Road. LONDON SE1 5BA

Cover Design by Covenant Publishing Team
Published by Covenant Publishing
Printed in the United Kingdom

TABLE OF CONTENT

ENDORSEMENTS

The book explores the duality of man's existence in the physical and spiritual realm at the same time. An understanding of this dynamic is required for successful living. It is said that you cannot take people to where you have not been. The author has offered insight from personal and ministerial experiences to help the reader navigate life successfully in the two realm.

Obafemi Omisade
National Overseer, New Covenant Church, UK

The perspective that one sees in this book is new and powerful. There are stones thrown at us by the wicked hands of men which we must do away with, whether or not we know about them. The recommendations in this book show that whatever stones may be blocking your progress can be dealt with if you know what to do as a child of God. Many think that they know how to handle stones but when you read this book you will catch a revelation of Christ from this uncommon perspective and you can be translated into living a higher life.

Concerning this title, I have had the privilege of both hearing it preached and also reading it. It is an amazing revelation of Jesus Christ that has come at this time to encourage every believer to see that God hates when His children are held back from reaching their destinies by hindrances. As many as receive the great message in this book and practice the injunctions derivable from it, shall live the overcomer's life.

Happy Reading.

Rev. Titus Ayoola Daniel
Pastor, New Covenant Church Leicester, UK

ACKNOWLEDGEMENT

For the gift of God, I am very grateful.

To my beautiful wife, Tola, I say a big thank you. To our children, you are God's perfect gifts, and I am very grateful.

To bring out this book and see beyond my humble beginnings, Bro Paul Jinadu, I am very grateful.

Baba Emmanuel Ajao, so much to thank God for your life and encouragement sir.

My wonderful congregation, you are the best, thanks a million.

Pastor Ayo Olufemi-Jotham, your contributions to make this a reality cannot be expressed in words. Pastor Sam O. Adewunmi, you are a gift to the church and to me personally. May God reward you. Akinyemi Adeshina, thanks for standing with me.

Engineer Remi Asuni, you are a friend and a father indeed. Chris Dele Folahanmi and Segun Makinde, thank you.

For every pulpit I have stood on to minister the word of God, thank you.

It's my Jubilee

DEDICATION

To Lolu Adegoke (TLR) – your message brought me
to the kingdom.

FOREWORD

As the saying goes: "A rolling stone gathers moss." Stones in your life, if left unchecked, will roll on down the years and can become a mountain. It is so important to give a new convert a detailed spiritual checkup, leaving no stone unturned. Stones that can easily be identified and removed by man soon after conversion can become mountains later in life that will take the might of an angel to remove.

You don't remove spiritual mountains by shouting at them. Even frequent fasting may not dislodge them. To get rid of them, they must be identified and named. Why? Because not all mountains are bad. Very often, Jesus went up the mountain to pray. He also gave the Sermon on the Mount. Jesus was transfigured on a mountain. Moses spent 40 days on the mountain fasting to receive the 10 commandments. The Bible is full of symbolisms of mountains.

The major difference between these mountains is that you stand on the good ones, while you are crushed under the bad ones. So we need education, and a thorough understanding of spiritual things to come out victorious.

This is why I can recommend this book by my son in the faith, Pastor Sayo. He has dug deep into the word and life's experiences to bring out these golden nuggets. I know he has the experience and success in the areas he outlined in 'Stones.' Just take the time to read the book. You may discover some stones you never thought you had. And you never know. As you read it, the truth can set you free, even without human hand.

Rev. Dr. Paul Jinadu
General Overseer, New Covenant Church

INTRODUCTION

INTRODUCTION

My knowledge of Geography taught me that a non-living object cannot respond to external stimuli. One of the most common examples of a non-living object is a stone. You may have heard the common expression, "as cold as a stone."

Looking through the Bible, there are so many instances where stones are mentioned. One of these passages is 1 Corinthians 10:4,

> *"And did all drink the same spiritual drink: for they drank of that spiritual rock that followed them: and that rock was Christ."*

It is interesting to note that Christ was referred to as a "rock." As a matter of fact, a moving Rock. This must be a mystery. How can a non-living object become mobile?

In another instance in Exodus 31:18 the Bible says,

> *"And he gave unto Moses, when he had finished speaking with him on Mount Sinai; He gave Moses the two tablets of testimony, tables of Stones, written with the finger of God."*

God used the stone as His slate to write His message to His people. This is very significant.

It was Joshua who threw more light on the importance of stones in Joshua 24:27.

> *"And Joshua said unto the people, behold this stone shall be a witness unto us, for it hath heard all the words of the Lord, which he spake unto us: it shall be therefore a witness unto you, lest Ye deny your God."*

This is a very bold and challenging comment from Joshua. The stone being a witness is strange because it is supposed to be a non-living being. How could a stone have heard what he was saying?

What explanation can be offered for a moving rock or stone that heard the words Joshua spoke to his people and was to be a witness? This is the point where we need to understand that the language of the Spirit is quite different from any other physically oriented day to day language.

It is important to note that in the Spirit realm, we operate like God who,

> *"Calls those things that be not as though they were" (Romans 4:17b).*

This is the explanation we have for some descriptions of the Bible referring to inanimate objects as though they have a life.

In the book of Zechariah 4: 7, the Bible says,

> *"Who are thou, o Great Mountain before Zerubbabel, thou shall become a plain."*

In this context, we understand that mountains, rocks or stones are referred to as challenges, problems, and situations.

The Bible says in Mark 11:23,

> *"For assuredly, I say to you, whoever says to this mountain, 'Be removed and be cast into the sea,' and does not doubt in his heart, but believes that those things he says will be done, he will have whatever he says."*

Here, the Bible is talking about mountain as a problem, a hinderance. We are encouraged from the spiritual point of view to speak to "our" mountains. Stones make up mountains and it is interesting to note that as long as they are hindrances in our lives, they are meant to be moved. These "mountains" are never designed to be permanent structures. By faith in God, we have been empowered to "shift" them.

No matter who may be going through the process of shame, this has never been recognised as a pleasant experience. This is the same with poverty or sickness. Some people have tried really hard but still experience more failures than successes. For such people, this could be very challenging. On the contrary, one of the things that keep life interesting is when we keep moving forward.

How Can A Mountain Be Moved?

As we earlier mentioned, Mark 11: 23 encourages us to speak to our mountains. As we know, mountains are in various shapes and sizes. A knowledge of the size of the mountain is usually beneficial to determine the amount of effort required to move the mountain.

The first category of stones we want to examine are stones that ordinary men can move.

CHAPTER ONE
STONES THAT ORDINARY MEN CAN MOVE

1

STONES THAT ORDINARY MEN CAN MOVE

"⁸ And the children of Israel did so, just as Joshua commanded, and took up twelve stones from the midst of the Jordan, as the Lord had spoken to Joshua, according to the number of the tribes of the children of Israel, and carried them over with them to the place where they lodged, and laid them down there. ⁹ Then Joshua set up twelve stones in the midst of the Jordan, in the place where the feet of the priests who bore the Ark of the Covenant stood; and they are there to this day" (Joshua 4:8-9).

Joshua was specifically instructed to speak to some men to carry a stone each on their shoulders into the midst of Jordan. Each man represented a tribe. For ease of reference, we shall refer to these stones as mountains. As we mentioned earlier, mountains are meant to be shifted. God spoke to Joshua of the necessity for these stones to be relocated from their original place to a site where they would fulfil purpose. However, for this to happen, Joshua would need help.

There are challenges like this in life. In order to overcome some life challenges and achieve purpose, we would need the help of men. God has already given specific instructions on how to overcome such obstacles and who to consult for the manifestation of this miracle. Therefore we do not need to despair. This sounds so simple but the story of the prodigal son illuminates the stumbling block along this process.

Be Around The Right People

Let us examine Luke 15:11–16 (NIV).

> "11 Jesus continued: "There was a man who had two sons. 12 The younger one said to his father, 'Father, give me my share of the estate.' So he divided his property between them. 13 "Not long after that, the younger son got together all he had, set off for a distant country and there squandered his wealth in wild living. 14 After he had spent everything, there was a severe famine

in that whole country, and he began to be in need. 15 So he went and hired himself out to a citizen of that country, who sent him to his fields to feed pigs. 16 He longed to fill his stomach with the pods that the pigs were eating, but no one gave him anything."

The last statement in the KJV reads, "… and no man gave unto him." Not giving to this young man was not because there were no men around him nor because they didn't have to give. It was just that they were not inclined to give. What an irony! For Joshua, he had men who were willing and ready to help him achieve his mandate, but for the prodigal, no man wanted to help.

Over the years I have realised that some miracles cannot happen without the help of men. Imagine the man that was taken with palsy in Luke 5:17-20.

"17 Now it happened on a certain day, as He was teaching, that there were Pharisees and teachers of the law sitting by, who had come out of every town of Galilee, Judea, and Jerusalem. And the power of the Lord was present to heal them 18 Then behold, men brought on a bed a man who was paralyzed, whom they sought to bring in and lay before Him. 19 And when they could not find how they might bring him in, because of the

crowd, they went up on the housetop and let him down with his bed through the tiling into the midst before Jesus. [20] *When He saw their faith, He said to him, "Man, your sins are forgiven you."*

This was a heroic act from friends to help a sick friend. It is encouraging to note that the healing of this sick man was not necessarily occasioned by his faith but by those of his friends. My prayer is that the Lord will help us in our times of need to locate such people who would be willing and ready to help us to remove our stones.

There are some problems that can be resolved quite easily with the right connections. If I am approached on a Sunday morning to help with food, I probably would not even need to pray. I believe this is a problem I can solve simply by dipping my hands into my pockets and provide a meal for such person. This is possible because God has provided me with the means to be able to help.

Our prayer requests for some issues should simply be to ask God to connect us with people who will help bring the mandate into manifestation. As the problem is mentioned to these people, and because they are led of God, they will be prepared to provide solutions. This has happened to me on several occasions.

A case in point occurred a while ago as I was contemplating changing my car. I believed God for a miracle and one afternoon, I went with a friend to a car showroom. At that point, the intention was not to buy a car but my friend, out of the goodness of his heart decided to pay for the vehicle we viewed. I ended up driving a new car home that same day. May God raise men to come to your aid in your time of need in the Name of Jesus.

Prayer Point

Ask God to grant you your own men that will be able to carry your stones. (God is preparing men to carry your stones).

CHAPTER TWO
STONES THAT GROUP OF MEN CAN MIRACULOUSLY MOVE

STONES THAT GROUP OF MEN CAN MIRACULOUSLY MOVE

It may be possible that certain stones exist that are too big for an individual to carry. These are stones that are bigger and heavier than those Joshua needed to move. An example of one of such stones is found in John 11:38-41.

> "38 *Jesus, once more deeply moved, came to the tomb. It was a cave with a stone laid across the entrance.* 39 *"Take away the stone," he said. "But, Lord," said Martha, the sister of the dead man, "by this time there is a bad odor, for he has been there four days."* 40 *Then Jesus said, "Did I not tell you that if you believe, you will see the glory of God?"* 41 *So they took away the stone."*

After the death of Lazarus, his body was placed in a tomb. A stone was required to close the entrance of the tomb to prevent the odour escaping. Men were required to roll this stone into place at the entrance of the tomb. Again, men were required when Jesus attended to raise Lazarus from the dead. Jesus instructed the men that were around to roll the stone away. What would have happened if there weren't men on site to carry out this instruction?

This would have been similar to what happened at the pool of Bethesda in John 5:1-7 (NIV),

> *"1 Sometime later, Jesus went up to Jerusalem for one of the Jewish festivals. 2 Now there is in Jerusalem near the Sheep Gate a pool, which in Aramaic is called Bethesda and which is surrounded by five covered colonnades. 3 Here a great number of disabled people used to lie – the blind, the lame, the paralyzed. 5 One who was there had been an invalid for thirty-eight years. 6 When Jesus saw him lying there and learned that he had been in this condition for a long time, he asked him, "Do you want to get well?" 7 "Sir," the invalid replied, "I have no one to help me into the pool when the water is stirred. While I am trying to get in, someone else goes down ahead of me."*

This man had concluded in his heart that he probably would not have stayed by the pool that long if he had helpers of destiny around him. He felt he was surrounded by the wrong crowd – people who were also very desperate for help. The blind is unable to help the blind cross the road. My prayer is that God will raise men and women to help you in your time of need, in Jesus name.

Let us paint a scenario of a Church trying to raise £200,000 pounds for a place to worship. Relying on just a person or family would be daunting but if the whole assembly believes in the vision and get behind it, we may find the task easier to achieve as the figure is simply re-distributed amongst many.

So we can see that we need men to help us carry mountains that may be too difficult for an ordinary person to carry. I have witnessed many miracles borne out of cooperation among men. The wall of Jerusalem was not built by Nehemiah alone. This task was achieved by the coming together of the Jews. My prayer is that God will touch the hearts of men to help when you call.

The Help Of God's Man

In some situations, God in His infinite wisdom may even choose to by-pass several men and handpick an individual knowing that some men may choose to be 'tired' when it comes to manual labour.

Let us look at Genesis 29:1-10 (KJV).

> *"1 Then Jacob went on his journey, and came into the land of the people of the east. 2 And he looked, and behold a well in the field, and, lo, there were three flocks of sheep lying by it; for out of that well they watered the flocks: and a great stone was upon the well's mouth. 3 And thither were all the flocks gathered: and they rolled the stone from the well's mouth, and watered the sheep, and put the stone again upon the well's mouth in his place. 4 And Jacob said unto them, my brethren, whence be ye? And they said, Of Haran are we. 5 And he said unto them, 'Know ye Laban the son of Nahor?' And they said, 'We know him.' 6 And he said unto them, 'Is he well?' And they said, 'He is well: and, behold, Rachel his daughter cometh with the sheep.' 7 And he said, 'Lo, it is yet high day, neither is it time that the cattle should be gathered together: water ye the sheep, and go and feed them.' 8 And they said, 'We cannot, until all the flocks be gathered together, and till they roll the stone from the well's mouth; then we water the sheep.' 9 And while he yet spake with them, Rachel came with her father's sheep; for she kept them. 10 And it came to pass, when*

Jacob saw Rachel the daughter of Laban his mother's brother, and the sheep of Laban his mother's brother, that Jacob went near, and rolled the stone from the well's mouth, and watered the flock of Laban his mother's brother."

In this instance, shepherds who were depended on to move the stone at the mouth of the well did so only when it suited them. On this particular day, Racheal was early to get to the well, and heaven was ready to remove the 'spirit of delay' in her life. God had empowered Jacob to remove the stone that was the object of delay. May the Lord send a Jacob that will accelerate the manifestation of the miracle you are waiting for.

Prayer Point

Pray that God will give you men who will stand before your vision, your ministry, and your life and will be there until the stone is rolled away.

STONES: RESCUED FROM SHAME

CHAPTER 3
STONES THROWN INTO ONE'S LIFE - 1

3

STONES THROWN INTO
ONE'S LIFE - 1

In this Chapter and the next, we will be looking at stones thrown into someone's life from two different angles. The first will focus on stones thrown by authority figures while the next will deal with stones thrown by people who have the authority handed to them. In both cases, as we will find out, stones can be thrown at us knowingly and unknowingly. The later chapter will end with steps on how people who have stones thrown at them can seek deliverance by the help of God.

Let us now look at the first scenario in this chapter.

Someone once said, "no one calls you a fool without your consent." It has also been said that "you are not a failure until you admit that you are." The journey to success in life is paved with hard work and determination, but also with the ingredient of "self-belief."

Curses Pronounced by Authority Figures

"Stones thrown into one's life" represent problems and issues constituted to serve as sources of ignorance in someone's life. For a very long time, generational curses and all sorts of family issues have kept many people down. Many are contending with issues as well as root causes of such issues and are struggling to understand these. Such problems or challenges are likened to stones that are thrown into one's life by another person, either ignorantly or consciously.

A typical example of this is found in Genesis 49:1-7 (KJV).

> "1 And Jacob called unto his sons, and said; Gather yourselves together, that I may tell you that which shall befall you in the last days. 2 Gather yourselves together, and hear, ye sons of Jacob; and hearken unto Israel your father. 3 Reuben, thou art my firstborn, my might, and the beginning of my strength, the excellency of dignity, and the excellency of power: 4 Unstable as water, thou shalt not excel; because thou wentest up to thy father's bed; then defiledst

thou it: he went up to my couch. 5 Simeon and Levi are brethren; instruments of cruelty are in their habitations. 6 O my soul, come not thou into their secret; unto their assembly, mine honour, be not thou united: for in their anger they slew a man, and in their self-will they digged down a wall. 7 Cursed be their anger, for it was fierce; and their wrath, for it was cruel: I will divide them in Jacob, and scatter them in Israel."

Jacob, who exercised the role of a father, decided to speak words into the lives of his children. He tailored his words in line with certain events that had occurred in the past. Reuben was his first born. In Hebrew tradition, being the first born is quite important and this child was entitled to a double portion of his father's inheritance. On top of this, Reuben had a lot of attributes already in his favour; excellency of dignity, excellency of power, and a man of might. In fact, the Amplified Bible put the qualities of Reuben in a very wonderful manner. He was described as "a man with pre-eminence of power and dignity." What an attribute! But with all these super attributes and qualities, Reuben was still a victim of instability, uncontrolled passion, and lack of self-discipline. This made his father pronounce words that shut his destiny.

While not in support of Reuben's behavioural deficiencies, I believe that we all go through different cycles in life. My opinion is that his father's punishment was too severe to the point that he was "stripped" of his position as the first born. This affected the generation after him – a group of people that did nothing wrong but to share the gene of Reuben. According to Hebrew history, it was claimed that there was not anybody of influence that came from the lineage of Reuben, even after many years.

The same thing applied to Simeon and Levi, when, out of revenge and anger, they killed many people to avenge their raped sister. In Genesis Chapter 49, Levi and Simeon were cursed by their father. Jacob pronounced on them that they would be scattered over Israel. The lineage of Simeon was practically wiped out of the history of Israel as a nation.

In Deuteronomy 33, when Moses began to bless the nation of Israel by reversing the curses that were placed on them by their father Jacob, the prayer of Moses for Reuben in verse 6 was very striking. Why did Moses speak those words? Why did his lineage have to pay for his men not being few? It was because the words of Jacob were already having a very adverse effect in the lineage of Reuben. Let us read the story from Deuteronomy 33:6-8,

"⁶ Let Reuben live, and not die; and let not his men be few. ⁷ And this is the blessing of Judah: and he said, Hear, Lord, the voice of Judah, and bring him unto his people: let his hands be sufficient for him; and be thou a help to him from his enemies. ⁸ And of Levi he said, Let thy Thummim and thy Urim be with thy holy one, whom thou didst prove at Massah, and with whom thou didst strive at the waters of Meribah."

Nothing was mentioned about Simeon anymore. What a disaster? Thank God for Moses, who pronounced a turn-around to the lineage of Levi. We should remember that Moses himself was a Levite. The words and deeds of Moses have proved to us that there is no negative situation or pronouncement that cannot be reversed.

Reversing Altered Destinies

Reuben, Simeon, and Levi could also have put things in place to reverse their father's destructive words that sealed their destinies.

Unfortunately, some people believe that destinies cannot be altered. If it took a man to curse Reuben, it definitely would take another man to bless him. From the Bible standpoint, I wonder what lesson Jabez learnt. Let us take a look at 1 Chronicles 4:10.

"10 And Jabez called on the God of Israel, saying, Oh that thou wouldest bless me indeed, and enlarge my coast, and that thine hand might be with me, and that thou wouldest keep me from evil, that it may not grieve me! And God granted him that which he requested."

He cried out to God for a change and God granted his request. He refused to explain or surrender his life to fate, as some of us would have done.

Another very good example of a man that will not settle for less is found in Genesis 28. This story became more fascinating in verse 30 when Isaac realised the mistake he made in blessing the wrong person. In this case, the blessing was irreversible. He politely advised Esau to accept his fate claiming that there were no blessings left for him. Life is all about bargaining. This was what Esau realised. So he was ready to bargain and fight, fight and bargain, refusing to take 'no' for an answer. He persistently and rigorously insisted that his father checked the reservoir for at least any residual blessing. He was not going to go Reuben's way of keeping silent and accepting fate. He challenged his father's sentence and did all that he could to provoke his father's blessing. Surprisingly, the father that said that there were no more blessings suddenly began to utter some words of blessing that were borne out of Esau's persistence and rugged determination.

"4 For whatsoever is born of God overcometh the world: and this is the victory that overcometh the world, even our faith" (1 John 5:4).

We Are Overcomers

We cannot afford to suffer like Abner who died like a fool.

He was too naive and trusting that he agreed to meet Joab at a secret location without any guard or weapons of self-defense or self-protection. He was not meant to sell himself that cheap with all the great battles he had seen and his years of experience with Saul and later Saul's son. He was expected to know better. Alas! His foolishness cost him his life. Abner performed below par. David was so furious and irritated with him that he called him a "fool" as described in 2 Samuel 3:30-33.

"30 So Joab, and Abishai his brother slew Abner, because he had slain their brother Asahel at Gibeon in the battle. 31 And David said to Joab, and to all the people that were with him, rend your clothes, and gird you with sackcloth, and mourn before Abner. And King David himself followed the bier. 32 And they buried Abner in

Hebron: and the king lifted up his voice, and wept at the grave of Abner; and all the people wept. [33] *And the king lamented over Abner, and said, Died Abner as a fool dieth?"*

Died Abner As A Fool Dies?

A.G. Brown's summation of Abner (2 Samuel 3:33) makes a very interesting reading on the paradox of his life.

"And the king lamented over Abner, and said, Died Abner as a fool dies?"

There are two or three different renderings of our text. Some take it thus – "Died Abner as a wicked man?" And then the answer is, "No, he did not. He fell by the foul hand of deliberate and deceitful murder." Others render the text – "Shall Abner die like a fool?" That is, "Shall he be unpitied? Shall his fall be unsung? Shall his murder be unrevenged?" There is a good deal to show for this rendering; because David, directly afterward, pronounces an awful imprecation on the house of Joab. But the third rendering, which we prefer, and which we shall take, is the one which we have here in our text: "Died Abner as a fool dieth?" 'That is, "Can it be true that such a man as Abner, with all his mental power and all his martial prowess - can it be true that Abner, of all men, died like a fool?" The next verse, you will see, explains the reference. His hands free, his feet, unfettered, and yet Abner the warrior falls down before the spear of Joab. "Died Abner as a fool dieth?" I think we may generally take for granted that in young manhood there is always a love of honest dealing. In fact, if anyone who calls himself a man objects to plain, straightforward dealing, the sooner he changes his name the better. Surely no young man in his senses will differ from us in the statement that no matter how successful a man may be in many aspects, yet his life is an utter failure if at the end he dies a fool's death. We recognize the fact that die we must. And I take it that, a true young man would far sooner face a fact like this, and would far sooner hear the preacher boldly deal with it than attempt the foolish task of escaping an unpleasant subject by not referring to it. What was the mark of folly about Abner's death?

Abner's Strange Simplicity And Wonderful Credulity

I do marvel at Abner - certainly, David did — that he, of all men, should have been so easily "gulled," for we know no other word that so exactly conveys the thought of our mind. Abner had been continually by the king's side. He must have known, therefore, that the art of political speaking is to conceal your thoughts, and that nature only gives courtiers' tongues to shroud by language the intentions of the heart. Strange that a man like Abner, who had passed through such a school as two courts, should have so readily believed the message which Joab sent him.

Now, is it not marvelous how unsuspicious men are of sin's designs? They are shrewd enough in other things. I have no doubt that many of you are sharp, keen, acute men of business. Your books will testify that you do not make very many bad debts. You can see through a man as quickly as most; yet how strange it is that often those who are shrewdest in other things are most deluded as to the nature of sin's designs!

As Homer describes in his Odyssey, there are the sirens on the rocks, who sing so sweetly that, if a Ulysses is to be kept from running his craft right on their rugged brows, the men must lash him to the mast and ply their oars with desperate earnestness, for the music of the sirens makes a deadly calm, and leaves no breath of air to fill the sails and take the vessel from her danger.

And so sin seems to sing like an enchantress; and the shrewdest and the cleverest men are irresistibly, almost imperceptibly, drawn toward it; and they who would see through a deception of another sort in a moment seem, like Abner, utterly blinded in this respect, What Satan raves to accomplish is to be revenged on God through God's creatures. Is it likely, then, that such a Joab as this can have any good intent when he says to thee by some sin, "Come, let us talk quietly in the gate?" And yet how willingly a man will turn aside with any sin! "A man is both ruined and saved through faith."

I confess that when first I heard that statement I was rather startled. I did not at first see its force, and I said, "Stay! There is a mistake. You mean that a man is saved through faith and is ruined by unbelief." The answer I received was: "That is true; so also is it that a man is either saved or lost by faith. If the faith be in God, through Christ, then that faith saves; but, on the other hand, if it is the faith which a man places in the representations made by Satan and sin, that faith damns him."

It was our first parents' faith in the words of the serpent that spread ruin over God's new-made world. And so I doubt not that there are many here concerning whom it may be said, as it was of Abner: "Shall that man die as the fool dieth? So keen in everything else, shall he be credulous enough to be led by so simple a snare as that set by the enemy?" Yet so is it.

Abner's Unusual Advantages

I think David specially thought of these when he burst out into the cry, "Died Abner as a fool died?"

You glean this from the 34th verse, "Thy hands were not bound, nor thy feet put into fetters." Abner was a prisoner to nobody but himself. No cord bound those mighty arms of his; no iron fetters were upon his feet; and yet he might as well have been born without hands or feet for all the good they were to him. Hands unused, feet unemployed, he stands still like a fool to be killed. Oh! Is it not so with many? I ask you, have not your advantages been unused? Let me ask thee, if thou weft to die and be lost wouldst thou not have to acknowledge that, in this respect, thou hast certainly played the fool, for. Thy, hands are not bound nor thy feet in fetters?

You are not bound with ignorance. It may be that there are some of you here who know the story of the gospel as well as the preacher. It may be that there are others of you here who could stand on this platform and run through all the main doctrines of the Word. What, and will you, with all this knowledge of the truth, yet die as the fool dieth - with unfettered feet and hands at liberty? I know not your history, but it would be a strange thing if there are not hundreds here who have been armed by holy precept.

Your Bible may be at the bottom of your box now, just as it was thrown in three years ago, when you left your home in the country. Not a few of you have been armed by noble examples. Have you not had a holy, noble, heavenly example in her who gave you birth, and who, perhaps, is at this moment before the throne? Then let me ask you, why die as a fool? If your hands be not bound, and you know the difference between right and wrong, if you have been armed by holy precept, and if you have been blessed with a heavenly example, why shall it ever be said of you, "Died Abner as a fool dieth?"

As Caesar Borgia lay dying fast he looked up, and, with clenched hands, muttered through his teeth the words, "I have provided for everything throughout life except death." And, doubtless, there are many here who can" take up Caesar Borgia's words as describing their own mad folly. Then, I ask you, if you die without hope, may it not be said as a requiem over you, "Died Abner as a fool dieth?"

Abner's Very Position Made The His Death The Greater

Oh, Abner, if you had refused to speak to Joab outside the city gates and insisted on entering them first, even Joab would not have dared to violate the sanctity of that citadel. Thou wouldst have been safe. I may be mistaken, but I think I am not. As far as my own feelings are concerned, the nearer a person is to safety when he dies the sadder is his death. It is sad enough for the sailor to go down in mid-Atlantic, when there are only the winds to howl his requiem, and when no eye looks down upon his struggles but that of the seagull whirling round and round upon the wings of the hurricane.

It is sad enough to sink down with only the shriek of the sea-bird in your ear; but, I think, it is sadder far to go down just outside the harbour's mouth, with a thousand eyes upon you and a thousand hands ready to help if they can. Sad enough for the traveller in the desert, parched with thirst and pinched with hunger, to lay him down in the burning dust to die, with only the vulture hovering over him in air which quivers with intensity of heat. But when we read some time back of one being literally starved to death in the great metropolis, when there were wealth all round, food in abundance and a thousand persons ready to vie with each other as to who should go to his rescue first, it seemed to me the climax of horror to die in the midst of plenty.

"Died Abner as a fool dieth" - credulous, with advantages unused, and on the very threshold of safety? God save us from such folly. Shall yonder Abner, who has been the child of prayer for thirty years, die a fool's death? Said a godly mother to a son who used to worship in this place, and is at the present time at the other end of the world, "Ah, my boy, if ever you get into perdition, it will be over ten thousand mother's prayers that she places in front of you as barriers."

It may be that there are some here who, though most deeply sunk in sin, yet know full well that there is no night nor morning but the cry goes up to heaven, "Lord, save my boy!" And shall Abner, the child of so many prayers, die the fool's death?

A. G. Brown - The Biblical Illustrator, Electronic Database. Copyright © 2002, 2003, 2006, 2011 by Biblesoft, Inc. All rights reserved.

I hope you also find this piece as interesting as I did. The whole idea is that we cannot continue to blame our failures on other people without taking full responsibility for our lives. Abner needed not to die if he was more careful with his life. In other words, we cannot continue to play the fool like Reuben, Simeon, and Levi. According to Isaiah 74:17, we need to fight.

> *"17 No weapon that is formed against thee shall prosper; and every tongue that shall rise against thee in judgment thou shalt condemn. This is the heritage of the servants of the Lord, and their righteousness is of me, saith the Lord."*

No stone thrown at you by the enemy must prosper – this summarises the scripture.

CHAPTER FOUR

STONES THROWN INTO ONE'S LIFE - 2

STONES THROWN INTO ONE'S LIFE - 2

Whenever I minister deliverance to someone, I understand the need to break all established covenants of past years. Over the years, I have identified three major types of covenants that need to be broken in order to experience complete freedom. These are:

1. Covenants entered into knowingly
2. Covenants entered into unknowingly
3. Covenants entered into on one's behalf

Often, we enter into covenants knowingly, but what then is a "covenant"? A covenant is a "formal agreement, contract or promise" between two parties according to the Oxford Dictionary. It has been observed that many do not give serious thought to contracts they enter into.

However, we also know that ignorance is no excuse for the consequences of contracts or covenants entered into. This is usually the opportunity the enemy preys upon. I know of a friend who signed as a guarantor on someone else's behalf without a full understanding of its implied ramifications until he found himself being arrested as his friend had defaulted. I am told he was imprisoned, therefore suffering for someone else's failure! How many times have we signed documents without a clear understanding of its implications?

Is there anything or situation in the spiritual realm that looks like this; the situations that we find ourselves because of our stupidity? Imagine the scenario of a young girl becoming "inadvertently" pregnant and because she is not ready, resorts to abortion. Some of the time, we see the abortion procedure going wrong and this may affect vital organs within her body which may have further future complications. In such situation, only the mercy of God can restore the damage.

Covenants Entered Into On Our Behalf

In the Garden of Eden Adam and Eve fell and disobeyed God's command. Today, the whole of the human race is suffering the consequences of their action. Let us look at the scriptures:

"12 Therefore, just as sin came into the world through one man, and death through sin, and so death spread to all men because all sinned — 13 for sin indeed was in the world before the law was given, but sin is not counted where there is no law. 14 Yet death reigned from Adam to Moses, even over those whose sinning was not like the transgression of Adam, who was a type of the one who was to come. 15 But the free gift is not like the trespass. For if many died through one man's trespass, much more have the grace of God and the free gift by the grace of that one man Jesus Christ abounded for many. 16 And the free gift is not like the result of that one man's sin. For the judgment following one trespass brought condemnation, but the free gift following many trespasses brought justification. 17 For if, because of one man's trespass, death reigned through that one man, much more will those who receive the abundance of grace and the free gift of righteousness reign in life through the one man Jesus Christ. 18 Therefore, as one trespass led to condemnation for all men, so one act of righteousness leads to justification and life for all men. 19 For as by the one man's

disobedience the many were made sinners, so by the one man's obedience the many will be made righteous. 20 Now the law came in to increase the trespass, but where sin increased, grace abounded all the more, 21 so that, as sin reigned in death, grace also might reign through righteousness leading to eternal life through Jesus Christ our Lord" (Romans 5: 12–21).

This offers an explanation as to how we all became sinners. Clearly, that was not our choice or deed. It all came about by the actions of one man, Adam.

The good news is that in verse 15, we also see how one man, Jesus of Nazareth, reversed the deeds of Adam! What a joy, what a relief! Yes, it was not our faults we became sinners in the first place, neither was it our doing we became saints.

There are many instances in the Bible that confirms that many are suffering not as a direct result of their actions but because of covenants sealed even before they were born. One of such cases was when David laid curses on Joab and his entire generation.

"Let it rest on the head of Joab, and on all his father's house; and let there not fail from the house of Joab one that hath an issue, or that is a leper, or that leaneth on a staff, or that falleth on the sword, or that lacketh bread" (2 Samuel 29).

What a disaster! Even unborn children were in trouble for the action of another! We thank the Lord for His promises of no longer visiting the iniquities of the father on sons anymore. Deuteronomy 24:16 says that,

> *"The fathers shall not be put to death for the children, neither shall the children be put to death for the fathers: every man shall be put to death for his own sin."*

This is echoed in Ezekiel 18:20 (NIV)

> *"Not share the guilt of the parent, nor will the parent share the guilt of the child. The righteousness of the righteous will be credited to them, and the wickedness of the wicked will be charged against them."*

We cannot thank God enough for the reversal of this pronouncement, but what about the damage that may have been done before the reality of this freedom?

There are also situations in life which we may not be able to pin down to covenants we have knowingly or unknowingly entered into. Let us search deeper.

Growing up back home in Africa, it was a common practice for my parents to visit Herbalists, Spiritual Centers, or Prayer Houses in order to seek spiritual protection over the children. At times, they would go on their own but sometimes, they would string us along with them. At those visits, we would be made to take along items of personal belongings to appease the "gods."

The Masquerade Took Over Our Destinies

A particular occasion which remains fresh in my mind was when my mother took us to the "shrine" of the family "masquerade" to receive "prayers." This was followed by the masquerade visiting our home for more sacrifices. For those who do not know, masquerades only pray to the "negative", i.e., pronouncing curses in the hope that such curses will turn to blessings. Such was the reality of our early childhood days and it was when we were growing up that we realised that what looked so simple was actually a significant ritual.

Later in life, I found myself been chased in my dreams by this same masquerade that prayed for us. It wasn't until I gave my life to Christ and I went through deliverance that this unfortunate incident became resolved in my life.

I wonder how many people may be in my former position.

Therefore, depending on the situation and circumstances that we find ourselves, we can use the following prayer line as a guide for us to deliver ourselves.

Prayer Of Deliverance

Dear Lord , I thank You today for Your mercies and faithfulness in my life, I stand before You today as Your child and I declare that I am born again and redeemed by the precious blood of Jesus.

I hereby declare that any covenant that I may have knowingly entered into, with the Devil (you can mention as many as you can remember), be nullified and cease to have effect in my life in Jesus name.

Dear Lord, I really want to thank You for destroying and nullifying all and any covenant that I may have entered into unknowingly at any given time in Jesus name. I declare by the reason of my redemption the effect of such also nullified in Jesus name.

Dear Lord, any covenant that may have been entered on my behalf. I henceforth disassociate myself from such in Jesus name.

From today I am free from all encumbrances and laws or traditions that violate my confession as a child of God because the Bible says in John 10:10,

"¹⁰ The thief cometh not, but for to steal, and to kill, and to destroy: I am come that they might have life, and that they might have it more abundantly."

I have life according to the word of God, I am free because John 8: 36 says,

"If the Son therefore shall make you free, ye shall be free indeed."

I am free indeed, Praise be to the Name of the Lord.

Amen.

CHAPTER 5
STONES THAT CANNOT BE ROLLED AWAY BY MEN

5

STONES THAT CANNOT BE ROLLED AWAY BY MEN

It is true that God can use individuals and sometimes groups of men to move stones away. However, it is also true that the best of men we still be a man. Medicine has greatly advanced and nearly every day we witness several breakthroughs in the field of medicine. There are myriads of problems that have in the past proved difficult but are now a thing of the past. However, without a shadow of a doubt, there still remain certain medical "stones" that the best of men cannot move or even attempt to move.

The account of the crucifixion of Jesus Christ is set in Mark 16:1-4.

"1 Now when the Sabbath was past, Mary Magdalene, Mary the mother of James, and Salome bought spices, that they might come and anoint Him. 2 Very early in the morning, on the first day of the week, they came to the tomb when the sun had risen. 3 And they said among themselves, "Who will roll away the stone from the door of the tomb for us?" 4 But when they looked up, they saw that the stone had been rolled away – for it was very large."

The greatest challenge faced by the women attending to anoint the body of Jesus was the issue of the stone that sealed the entrance of the tomb. This is better described in Mathew's account in Mathew 27:57-60.

"57 When it was evening, there came a rich man from Arimathea, named Joseph, who also was a disciple of Jesus. 58 He went to Pilate and asked for the body of Jesus. Then Pilate ordered it to be given to him. 59 And Joseph took the body and wrapped it in a clean linen shroud 60 and laid it in his own new tomb, which he had cut in the rock. And he rolled a great stone to the entrance of the tomb and went away."

Here we are given an account of how the tomb was cut out of a rock and the fact that a great stone was *rolled,* not carried, to secure the entrance. For a clearer picture of what happened here, we need to understand how and why such a stone was required at the tomb of Jesus.

- Joseph of Arimathea the original owner of the tomb was a very rich man so the likelihood of him been buried with a lot of valuables was quite high. Some Jews believed in life after death and therefore made provision for needs in the afterlife.

- To reduce the risk of vandalism and theft.

- The tomb was cut in a way that the stone at the entrance was engineered to roll down and stop at the entrance or mouth of the tomb and by doing this it would have been impossible for anyone to move the stone away. In the case of the Lord, Matthew 27 actually highlighted the uniqueness of the body of Christ.

The Guard At The Tomb

As if the stone was not hindrance enough, they also set a seal and set a guard, which would have discouraged anyone from tampering with the stone. Any attempts to unroll the stone carried with it the risk of the wrath of the guards and indeed, the Jewish authority. This literally killed off any potential help from man. As terminal as this situation looked, I am gladdened because it is a readymade case for God to step into. Let's look at verses 62-66 of Matthew 27.

> "62 *The next day, that is, after the day of Preparation, the chief priests and the Pharisees gathered before Pilate* 63 *and said, 'Sir, we remember how that impostor said, while he was still alive, 'After three days I will rise.'* 64 *Therefore order the tomb to be made secure until the third day, lest his disciples go and steal him away and tell the people, 'He has risen from the dead,' and the last fraud will be worse than the first.'* 65 *Pilate said to them, 'You have a guard of soldiers. Go, make it as secure as you can.'* 66 *So they went and made the tomb secure by sealing the stone and setting a guard."*

So what happened to this particular stone?

Angelic Assistance

Matthew 28:1-4 says,

> "1 *Now after the Sabbath, toward the dawn of the first day of the week, Mary Magdalene and the other Mary went to see the tomb.* 2 *And behold, there was a great earthquake, for an angel of the Lord descended from heaven and came and rolled back the stone and sat on it.* 3 *His appearance was like lightning, and his*

clothing white as snow. ⁴ And for fear of him the guards trembled and became like dead men."

What seemed impossible by the best of men was dealt with by a single angel of the Lord. Heaven decided to visit the earth and the powers on earth gave way – glory be to God. There wasn't even the mention of the seal being broken or the guards that were assigned to monitor the rock faking their deaths.

It didn't end there – the angel that rolled away the stone turned the stone into a chair, waiting for anyone to challenge his authority. Look at Romans 8:31,

"What shall we then say to these things? If God be for us, who can be against us?"

That explains my boldness and confidence to declare that all the mountains before you are going to be moved either by man or Angel.

In 2 Kings 19:35-36 the Bible says,

"³⁵ And it came to pass on a certain night that the angel of the Lord went out, and killed in the camp of the Assyrians one hundred and eighty-five thousand; and when people arose early in the morning, there were the corpses — all dead. ³⁶ So Sennacherib king of Assyria departed and went away, returned. home, and remained at Nineveh."

One angel went after a whole troop of soldiers and single-handedly killed 185,000 soldiers in one single night. This demonstrates the awesome power of God and how Heaven chooses to intervene in the affairs of men here on earth.

Angelic ministry is for every believer

One questions that keep coming up in my heart are these: "Am I qualified to engage the ministry of angels in my life struggles, and how can I?"

Looking closely into the word of God in Hebrews 1:14, we see,

> "14 *Are not all angels ministering spirits sent to serve those who will inherit salvation?"*

So angels are actually ministers. Each time they carry out an assignment, they are simply doing what they are meant to do.

Angels are not to be worshipped

Some years back in the course of ministry, I came in contact with a lady who claimed that she sees angels all around her bedroom. I asked her to describe what she saw. She said they were very short and that they were always dancing around her bed. I quickly pointed out to her that she has been deceived as the description of what she saw is not in any way true to the scriptural definition of an angel of the Lord as in Joshua 5:13-14.

> " 13 *Now it came about when Joshua was by Jericho, that he lifted up his eyes and looked, and behold, a man was standing opposite him with his sword drawn in his hand, and Joshua went to him and said to him, "Are you for us or for our adversaries?" 14 He said, "No; rather I indeed come now as captain of the host of the LORD." And Joshua fell on his face to the earth, and bowed down, and said to him, "What has my lord to say to his servant?"*

Most times when men see angels they are prone to want to offer worship because of the awesomeness of their appearance. This is due to the fact that they are celestial beings who stay close to the throne of The Almighty. In Acts 10:3-4, we read,

> "3 *He saw in a vision evidently about the ninth hour of the day an angel of God coming in to him, and saying unto him, Cornelius. 4 And when he looked on him, he was afraid, and said, what is it, Lord? And he said unto him, thy prayers and thine alms are come up for a memorial before God."*

Cornelius referred to the angel as 'Lord', before realizing he was an angel. Daniel in the book that bears his name, in Chapter 8:16-17, was so frightened when he saw an angel. The presence was so overwhelming that he fell on his face out of fear. What a sight?

> *"I heard the voice of a man between the banks of Ulai, and he called out and said, "Gabriel, give this man an understanding of the vision." So he came near to where I was standing, and when he came I was frightened and fell on my face; but he said to me, "Son of man, understand that the vision pertains to the time of the end" (NASB).*

Angels excel in strength

I had an encounter so many years back in my journey of faith. I was in a place all by myself. As I was praying, suddenly, a very strange looking man "floated" into the room. When he came in, I was so afraid and all the hair on my body stood up. I was so overwhelmed that I could not even utter a word. I did not recover until this creature left. This creature seemed tall and fit, with fiery red eyes and he was barefooted. He could not have been a normal human being. My guess is that he was an angel.

Angels are not weak beings - they are strong. They excel in strength - what a blessing? Psalm 103:20 says,

"Bless the LORD, ye his angels that excel in strength, that do his commandments, hearkening unto the voice of his word."

Do not pray to angels

There is not a single verse of scripture that encourages us to pray to angels. They are ministers to the heirs of salvation but they are not to be ordered around or commanded by the heirs. God sends His angels to achieve His purpose in our lives.

Haggai was not even aware when God sent an angel to protect Ishmael in Genesis 21:17,

"17 And God heard the voice of the lad; and the angel of God called to Hagar out of heaven, and said unto her, what aileth thee, Hagar? Fear not; for God hath heard the voice of the lad where he is."

Angels carry out God's word

Angels do not have a will of their own. They simply obey the voice of The Lord. They carry out God's intention with passion and they will do everything to see that the counsel of heaven is enforced here on earth. From the pages of the scripture, we realize that angels hearken to the voice of God. This is clearly explained in the interaction between Zechariah and Angel Gabriel in Luke 1:19,

"And the angel answered him, "I am Gabriel. I stand in the presence of God, and I was sent to speak to you and to bring you this good news."

Therefore, every time we quote the word of God, which is the Bible, we are speaking the language that angels can understand. For example, the scriptures declare in Philippians 4:19.

"But my God shall supply all your need according to his riches in glory by Christ Jesus."

With this scripture, we are setting angels on assignment to supply our needs because we are looking up to God and because God will not disappoint us, He will have to send the angels to deliver our request to us. This is further collaborated in Genesis 28:12-13,

"12 And he dreamed, and behold a ladder set up on the earth, and the top of it reached to heaven: and behold the angels of God ascending and descending on it. 13 And, behold, the LORD stood above it, and said, I am the LORD God of Abraham thy father, and the God of Isaac: the land whereon thou liest, to thee will I give it, and to thy seed."

The angels were ascending with the prayers of the saints and descending with the answers from God, who is the answer to all of our needs.

This is also highlighted so strongly in Daniel 10:12-14 (KJV).

> *"12 Then said he unto me, 'Fear not, Daniel: for from the first day that thou didst set thine heart to understand, and to chasten thyself before thy God, thy words were heard, and I am come for thy words. 13 But the prince of the kingdom of Persia withstood me one and twenty days: but, lo, Michael, one of the chief princes, came to help me; and I remained there with the kings of Persia. 14 Now I am come to make thee understand what shall befall thy people in the latter days: for yet the vision is for many days.'"*

From the first day Daniel prayed, God answered his prayers. What a great God we serve?

Angels Are Real

With the little I have seen here on earth, I can argue that angels are real and relevant to our world today. There are several stones men are struggling with today, but no matter how challenging these situations may seem, God is able to move them through His angels.

In my ministry, I have come across some very challenging situations and so many times I am humbled by the graciousness and mighty manifestation of God's divine hand.

Ten years ago, there was a day we were at Church and during the course of ministry, I remember asking the congregation to pray against the spirit of death and I also vividly remember asking all the elderly people in the Church to come out for prayers. We prayed and laid hands on them.

Later on that very day, one of our young men went out to play football and before we knew it, he slumped and to my amazement blood was oozing from every part of his body. He went from a position of being in good physical shape to requiring surgery. It was a scary sight, but hard as the surgeons tried, they could not locate the source of the hemorrhage. Each time he was opened up, the flow of the blood was stemmed but as soon as he was covered up, the flow would start again. He was transferred from one hospital to another until they decided to call for pastoral support as it seemed death was inevitable.

As prayers were being offered, it seemed his life was being restored. He began to respond to treatment to the utter surprise of the medical staff. To the glory of God, the young man is today a graduate with a Master of Science degree. He is hale and hearty.

With God, there is no battle that cannot be won. We serve a God of wonders. Someone once asked me for a definition of wonder. My response was and still is, "whatever causes you to wonder is definitely a wonder"

My Stone Of Barrenness

My wife and I got married and we were hopeful of starting a family without any stress. After our first year of marriage, we travelled out of Nigeria to the United Kingdom hoping for the fruit of the womb within another year at the longest. After the third year in the United Kingdom, we chose to be examined by our doctors. Things got so bad we became a regular Church "prayer point"

On one of our visits to the Gynecologist, we were told to return within three months and that by then, our story should have changed. Nothing happened. It seemed our last hope was IVF but even so, we were told nothing was guaranteed.

I remember on one of such days, standing in the place of prayer, I fell into a trance where I saw a room filled with lots of people. All were women sitting down and one after the other a nurse would come and call the next patient into a place that looked like the labour ward. On this particular occasion, she came out and called my wife's name and I came back from the trance. I told my wife what I had seen and declared that the barrenness was over. It was that same year, our seventh year of marriage, that we were blessed with a wonderful Marvelous gift, for which we are ever grateful. When God stepped in, we did not have to go through the IVF. What a God of wonder?

Your stone will move when God steps in.

Healed Of Cancer

In one of my messages, I spoke about the healing power of God. I made mention of certain cases which sounded big and I can also remember making particular reference to cancer. Not only did I mention cancer, I also mentioned a specific cancer and I claimed that God can terminate and heal such completely. After the service I expected everybody to go home but to my amazement, a particular couple remained glued to their chairs.

I approached them and the husband said to me that they were in shock as, a week before that day, they were in the hospital and the Doctor diagnosed the wife as having the particular cancer I mentioned during my preaching. They also said they had agreed not to share this with anyone as they needed time to digest what they had heard and what they were to do. Hearing that particular kind of cancer mentioned from the pulpit drew all sorts of emotions for them. We burst into praise knowing fully well that whatever man cannot handle, God is more than able to.

I encouraged them to go and see the surgeon and to continue with their treatment. Shortly after, the lady was invited for surgery to remove the cancerous cells. I decided to attend on the day of the operation to encourage the couple but just as was declared by God, as the procedure commenced, the doctors announced that miraculously, the lady was now cancer free. What?

God Visited Her Work Place

There was another lady that had a serious challenge at work. She was being discriminated against. Those she had trained were being promoted before her. Although she took her case to employment tribunal several times, she kept losing. She did not want to go back to work with these people. Later on, she took the case up with a Barrister and the company settled out of court. She applied to another organization and got double the pay she was previously on. Where men found it difficult to help her, God brought heaven down to help.

I can go on and on about the manifestations of the grace of our God. This should not surprise anyone that has come to accept and relate to God as El-Shaddai. For such people, miracles are inevitable.

I'd like to include an excerpt from an article on the name El-Shaddai.

El Shaddai

Pronounced el shad-dY', this is the best-known of the "El" compound names. It means The All-Sufficient One and is usually translated in English Bibles as "God Almighty", "the Almighty" or "Almighty God". The exact derivation of the word "Shaddai" is not known. According to my research, all of the following words have been used at various times in the development of the name:

The Hebrew word "dai" (meaning "sheds forth", "pours out", or "to heap benefits") suggests provision, sustenance, and blessing. Thus, God is the All-Sufficient, All-Bountiful El. (Genesis 42:24-25)

The Hebrew word "shad" or "shadayim" (meaning "breast" or "breasts") occurs 24 times as "Shaddai" and signifies One who nourishes, supplies and satisfies (Isaiah 60:16, 66:10-13). Combined with the word for God, "El", it then becomes the "One mighty to nourish, satisfy, and supply".

The Hebrew root word "shadad" (meaning "to overpower" or "to destroy") suggests absolute power. While Elohim is the God who creates, in the name "Shaddai" God reveals Himself as the God who compels nature to do what is contrary to itself. He is able to triumph over every obstacle and all opposition; He is able to subdue all things to Himself.

An Akkadian word "Šadu" (meaning "mountain"), suggests great strength.

All of these names - whether individually or collectively - naturally would be intensified when combined with "El" and would refer to YHWH as the One who mightily nourishes, satisfies, protects, and supplies His people. El Shaddai is our All-Sufficient Sustainer. It is God as "El" who helps, and it is God as "Shaddai" who abundantly blesses with all manner of blessings.

As Nathan Stone wrote: "...the idea of One who is all-powerful and all-mighty is implied . . . for only an all-powerful One could be all-sufficient and all-bountiful. He is almighty because He is able to carry out His purposes and plans to their fullest and most glorious and triumphant completion. . . . So He is able to save to the uttermost. And He is able to do exceedingly abundantly above all that we can ask or think."

To experience God's sufficiency, we must realize our own insufficiency

The name "Shaddai", by itself, occurs 41 times in the Old Testament, 29 times in Job alone, and is translated "Almighty" in most English Bibles. In fact, the name "Shaddai" is the one written on the Mezuzah scroll.

Genesis 49:25 — "from the El of your father who helps you, and by the Almighty [Shaddai] who blesses you with blessings of the heavens above, blessings of the deep that lies beneath, blessings of the breasts and of the womb" (TS98).

Job 5:17 — "Look, blessed is the man whom Eloah does reprove, so do not despise the discipline of the Almighty" (TS98).

Job 33:4 — "It is the Spirit of God that made me, the breath of Shaddai that gives me life" (CJB).

Psalm 91:1 — "He who dwells in the secret place of the Most High [Elyon] Will rest in the shadow of the Almighty [Shaddai]" (WEB).

Isaiah 13:6 — "Howl, for the day of YHWH is near! It comes as a destruction from the Almighty [Shaddai]" (TS98).

See also Numbers 24:4, 16; Ruth 1:20,21; Job 6:4, 6:14, 8:3-5, 11:7, 13:3, 15:25, 21:15,20 22:3, 22:17, 22:23-26, 23:16, 24:1, 27:2, 27:10-13, 29:5, 31:2, 31:35, 32:8, 34:10,12, 35:13, 37:23, 40:2; Psalm 68:14; Ezekiel 1:24; Joel 1:15.

The compound name "El Shaddai" first appears is in Genesis 17:1: — "When Avram [Abraham] was 99 years old Adonai appeared to Avram and said to him,

'I am El Shaddai [God Almighty]. Walk in my presence and be pure-hearted'" (CJB).

And one particular passage that employs both "El" alone and the compound "El Shaddai" is Genesis 49:24-25 — "but his bow remained taut; and his arms were made nimble by the hands of the Mighty One (El) of Ya'akov (Jacob), from there, from the Shepherd, the Stone of Isra'el, by the God [El] of your father, who will help you, by El Shaddai, who will bless you with blessings from heaven above, blessings from the deep, lying below, blessings from the breasts and the womb" (CJB).

Further passages in the Old Testament that use the name "El Shaddai":

Genesis 28:3 — "May El Shaddai bless you, make you fruitful and increase your descendants, until they become a whole assembly of peoples" (CJB).

Genesis 35:11 — "And Elohim said to him, 'I am El Shaddai. Bear fruit and increase, a nation and a company of nations shall be from you, and sovereigns come from your body'" (TS98).

Exodus 6:3 — (God spoke to Moses...)"'I appeared to Avraham, Yitz'chak (Isaac) and Ya'akov (Jacob) as El Shaddai, although I did not make myself known to them by my name, Yud-Heh-Vav-Heh (YHWH) [Adonai]'" (CJB).

See also Genesis 43:14, 48:3; Numbers 24:4,16; Ruth 1:20,21; Job 5:17, 6:14, 8:3,5, 11:7, 13:3, 15:25, 21:15,20, 22:3,17,23-26, 23:16, 24:1, 27:2,10-13, 29:5, 31:2,35, 32:8, 33:4, 34:12, 35:13, 37:23, 40:2; Psalm 68:14; Isaiah 13:6, 60:15,16, 66:10-13; Ezekiel 1:24, 10:5; Joel 1:15.

It's important to note here that to experience God's sufficiency as our all-sufficient El Shaddai, we must realize our own insufficiency. To experience God's fullness as He has revealed Himself through His names, we must first empty ourselves — that is, make ourselves empty vessels which El Shaddai can then fill and use.

I have come to realize that it takes the combination of men and the power of God to live a fulfilled and accomplished life. David had this to say in Psalm 18:28-29,

"28 For thou wilt light my candle: The Lord my God will enlighten my darkness. 29 For by thee I have run through a troop; and by my God have I leaped over a wall."

I definitely can make it with You by my side, and trust Your words that say in Deuteronomy 31:5-6,

"5 The LORD will deliver them up before you, and you shall do to them according to all the commandments which I have commanded you. 6

"Be strong and courageous, do not be afraid or tremble at them, for the LORD your God is the one who goes with you. He will not fail you or forsake you."

In this, we can trust His promises are true.

Prayer Points

- We need to appreciate God's faithfulness and mercies over the years.

- Bless God for the many people He had moved to be of help to you at different times over the years.

- Appreciate God for moving your mountains even when you really did not ask Him to move them.

- Let us look at all the mountains and speak like Zechariah, "Who are thou, O great mountain? Before Zerubbabel thou shalt become a plain: and he shall bring forth the headstone thereof with shoutings, crying, Grace, grace unto it" (Zechariah 4:6).

- Let us trust God for the grace of favour and believe that those Stones that needed men to move, God will inspire men to move them and also those Stones that needed angels to move, God will send Angels to move them.

- That God will raise men that will stand by you.

- That God will raise a group of men that will stand by you.

- That God will grant you divine help. Where men cannot go, angels can go without any scratch.

www.ingramcontent.com/pod-product-compliance
Lightning Source LLC
Chambersburg PA
CBHW070549030426
42337CB00016B/2419